ZOOM MADE EASY

A Complete Guide to setting up your Zoom
For Education, Video Conferencing, Virtual
Meetings, Webinar and Live Stream

Daniel B. Smith

Independent Publisher

CONTENTS

INTRODUCTION

Zoom serves organizations of all industries and sizes because their platform can be flexibly scale to fit any user count and budget. But one of the coolest parts of our jobs is seeing just how much of an impact Zoom can have on small businesses.

However, some individual and organization are finding it hard setting up their Zoom account and other Zoom's features. This is why this book is here to guide and educate users on how to set up their Zoom account perfectly.

Meanwhile, before we proceed, here are some benefits of Zoom App and Why I recommend it for business owners both large and small scale business.

There are challenges that are unique to running a small business, for instance executing multiple processes with just a few people and limited budget, and prioritizing the time and resources to make it all happen efficiently — that can be solved with the Zoom platform. Why? Because Zoom provides easy-to-use video communications that empower people to accomplish more.

Communications should help every growing business achieve its goals, but also help meet its constantly evolving needs. Zoom's simplicity and ease of use, not to mention its tiered pricing and usage plans, simplify how small-business teams manage their time, enhance productivity, and scale the company.

Zoom helps you do just that with a ton of video communications capabilities packed into one low monthly price. Our integrations with Google and Microsoft will streamline your meetings, and our App Marketplace has over 200 integrations with leading apps like Slack and PayPal to extend the power of Zoom.

Other Benefits:

- Modern and easy communications for your dispersed

team
- Single platform for meetings, phone, webinars & chat
- The best value and return on investment
- Free for Light Users
- Boosts Productivity

CHAPTER 1 - BRIEF DETAILS ABOUT ZOOM

WHAT IS ZOOM?

Zoom is a cloud-based video conferencing tool with a local, desktop client and a mobile app that lets you host virtual one-on-one or team meetings easily. Meanwhile, with Zoom special features such as the powerful audio, video and collaboration features, this online remote communication tool connects remote team members with each other.

BRIEF HISTORY ABOUT ZOOM

Zoom Video Communications Incorporation, which can be simply called Zoom is an American communications technology company that has its headquartered in San Jose, California. A former Cisco Webex engineer and executive, Eric Yuan established Zoom in the year 2011. However, he officially launched its software in the 2013.

Zoom was established with the major aim of providing videotelephony and online chat services through a cloud-based peer-to-peer software platform and also use for teleconferencing, telecommuting, distance education, and social relations. Zoom became a unicorn company in the year, 2017 due to its massive revenue growth, and reliability of the software.

ZOOM SPECIAL FEATURES

Zoom provides special features for its users, who can choose to record sessions, collaborate on projects, and share or annotate on one another's screens, all with one easy-to-use platform. One of Zoom's key strengths is its simplicity, but this does not mean that the platform is without a variety of advanced features that remote workers will find useful for improving their productivity.

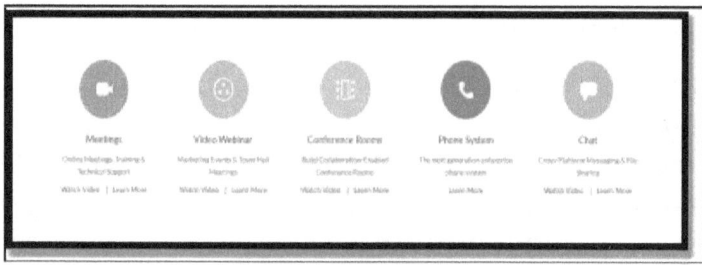

Zoom's key features include:

- HD video chat and conferencing
- Audio conferencing using VoIP (Voice over Internet Protocol)
- Instant messaging
- Virtual backgrounds for video calls
- Screen sharing and collaborative whiteboards
- Hosting video webinars

Zoom's special features focus on providing an easier to use product than competitors, as well as cost savings, which include minimizing computational costs at the infrastructure level and having a high degree of employee efficiency.

CHAPTER 2 - GETTING STARTED ON ZOOM

ZOOM COMPACTIBILITY

Zoom platform is compatible with Windows, iOS, Mac, Android, and Linux. However, the layout is slightly different depending on whether you are on desktop or mobile.

ZOOM PLAN

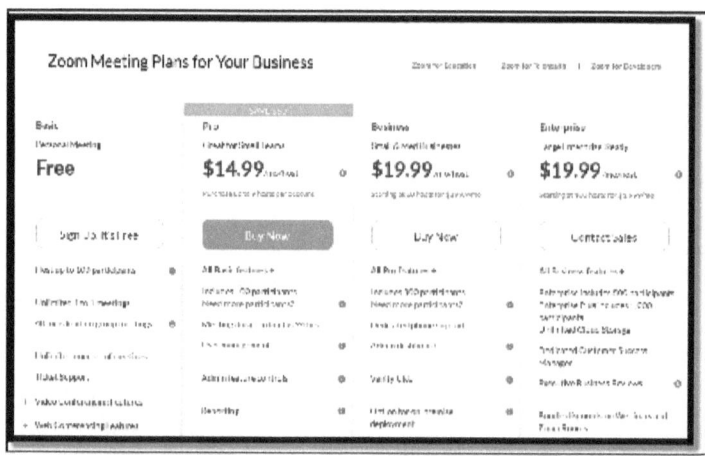

There are four plans offered by Zoom with their different pricing plans to suit your specific needs;

1. **Basic Plan:** This is the free and most popular plan, in which virtual meetings can be held with up to 100 participants, unlimited one-on-one meetings, and meetings with multiple participants can be held for up to 40 minutes. (When your time is up, you can simply restart a meeting if need be). The free option also allows users to conduct meetings in HD video

and with audio, participants can join via their PC or a telephone line, and both desktops and apps can be shared. In summary, the basic plan host up to 100 participants, plus unlimited one-on-one meetings, plus video conferencing, plus screen sharing, plus local recording, and scheduling via Chrome extensions.

2. **Pro Plan:** This plan costs $14.99/month per host. It also includes all "Basic" features with additional usage reports and 1 GB cloud storage.

3. **Business Plan:** This plan costs $19.99/month per host. It also includes all "Pro" features with additional supports up to 300 participants and admin dashboard.

4. **Enterprise Plan:** This plan costs $19.99/month per host. It also includes all "Business" features with additional supports up to 500 participants and unlimited cloud storage.

DOWNLOAD ZOOM

It is very possible to join a meeting just from your browser, but in the interests of longevity and avoiding browser limitations, It's simply best you should download the application.

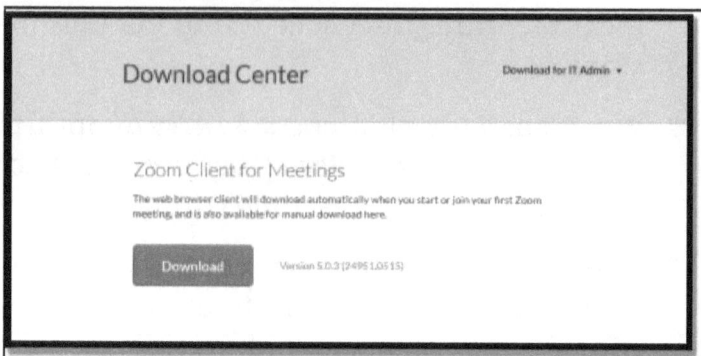

HOW TO DOWNLOAD THE ZOOM APP

1. **Using Desktop:** Start by clicking on the Link https://zoom.us/download. Then Click the blue button "Download" to access the installer. Then, proceed to open the Zoom installer from your Downloads folder and follow the on-screen steps to set up your Zoom Client.

2. **Using Mobile Devices:** For iOS users, download and install the Zoom iOS from the App Store while Android Users are to download and install the app from the App Store.

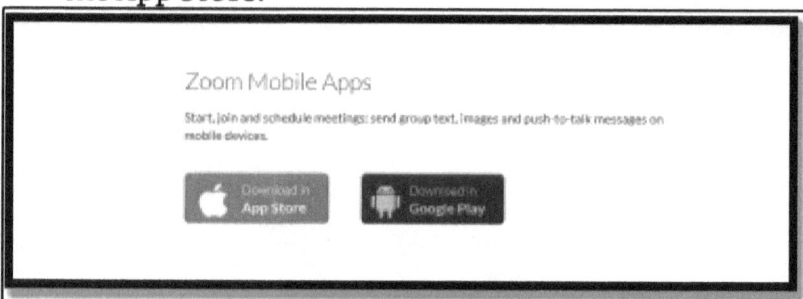

3. **Using Chromebook:** Download and install the Zoom

app through the Chrome Web Store.

Also, there are various plugins available including a Google Chrome extension, Mozilla Firefox extension, Microsoft Outlook plugin, and IBM Notes plugin. If you will be using Zoom for the foreseeable future for work purposes, you may want to download and install appropriate add-ons now.

HOW TO SIGN UP FOR ZOOM

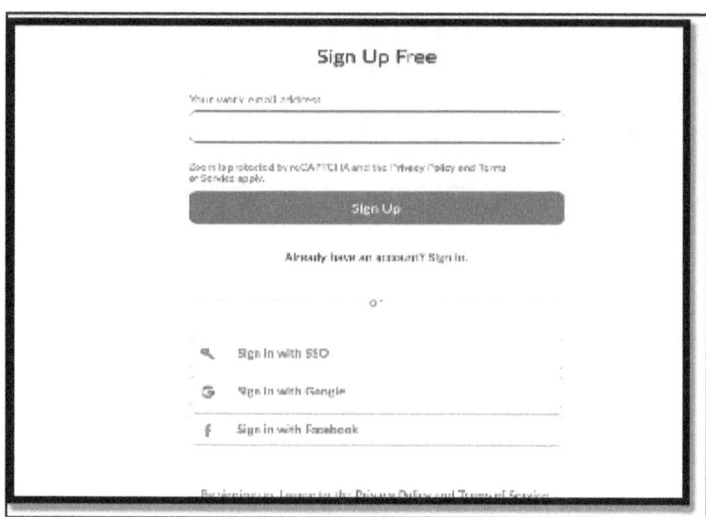

Since you have downloaded and installed the Zoom App, the next is to sign up as a first time user. But if you have already sign up earlier, just proceed by signing in.

1. **Using Desktop**: You begin by heading to their website - https://zoom.us and click on the blue "Sign Up" button that's at the top-right corner of the screen. However, there are few available options when it comes to signing up for Zoom account. You can either create your zoom account using email address, SSO (Single Sign-On) or using your social media account (that's sign up through either Google or Facebook) as seen on the photo above.

Then Zoom will send a confirmation link through your email. Click on that link to activate your account. (**screenshot email**) Then at the next stage, you will need to complete your account creation with your name and a strong password. (**csreenshot from phone**)

If you wish, on the next screen, you can invite your colleagues other administrators or staff members to also create their own account, you can enter their email addresses & select the "I am not a robot" checkbox. If not, click "Skip this step."(**screenshot administrator**)

2. **Using Mobile Device:** Now that you have downloaded the app on your mobile device, proceed to Sign up to Zoom by following the same procedure that are similar to the desktop process.

You can then proceed to sign in to Zoom.

Sign In

Email Address

Email Address

Password

Password   Forgot password?

Zoom is protected by reCAPTCHA and the Privacy Policy and Terms of Service apply.

Sign In

☑ Stay signed in   New to Zoom? Sign Up Free

ZOOM EXTRA SETTING

However, before we proceed to Zoom Meeting, there are extra settings you need to fix in perfect place, ensure that the correct settings are enabled and that you know how to create and launch a meeting.

Using Zoom Web Portal

- Profile Setting: When using the web portal, you first head over to the Zoom website, click on "Your Account" in the top-right to manage your profile. You can change details under the "Profile" tab such as your name, picture, default meeting ID, password and time zone.

- Default Settings: Next is to head over to "Settings." Here, you can adjust settings implemented by default, including whether or not video is automatically enabled when you or participants join a meeting; whether or not participants can join a scheduled meeting before the host arrives.

- Password Settings: In the interests of security and to prevent scammers from hijacking a meeting, you should endeavour to use strong passwords.

Passwords were not always enabled by default, but after Zoom founder Eric Yuan apologized for "falling short of the community's -- and our own -- privacy and security expectations," a rush of security changes were made, including the enabling, by default, of passwords for scheduled, instant, and personal meetings.

- Audio Settings: Next up is audio type, you can pick telephone and computer audio or one or the other to be automatically permitted. However, given the rapid rise of users, Zoom has warned:

"Due to increased demand, dial-in by phone audio conferencing capabilities may be temporarily removed from free Basic account[s]. During this time, we strongly recommend using our computer audio capabilities."

- Permission Settings: You can also decide whether or not to allow public and private chats when you host a meeting; you can give permission for files to be transferred, and who can share their screen -- just the host, or participants, too.

There are other, more advanced controls, but these are the main settings you should be aware of for now.

Using Zoom Desktop/Mobile App

The Zoom desktop app has a similar layout, with "Settings" accessible from the top-right corner. The options you can access here are related to your PC, such as whether or not you want to use dual monitors or automatically enter a full-screen mode when a meeting starts. Meanwhile, you can also test your microphone and speaker setup, choose a color theme, select a default location for recordings, and tweak accessibility controls, among other functions.

HOW TO SET UP THE ZOOM MEETINGS

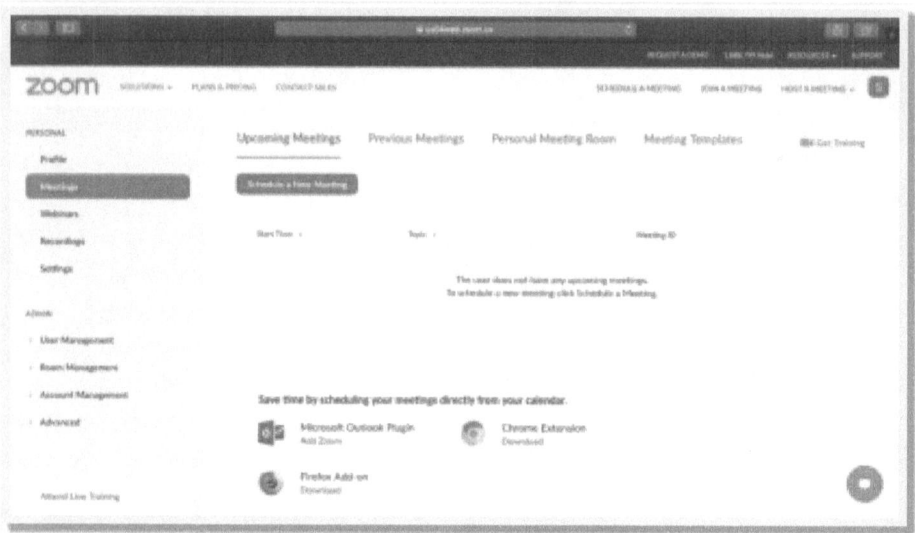

Setting up a Zoom meeting isn't sky rocket; it's quite easy to set up with the procedure provided in this book. Here's a step-by-step guide to setting up the Zoom Meetings and the app makes it super easy for anyone to set up and conduct virtual meetings.

USING DESKTOP (Starting A Zoom Meeting)

STEP 1: Set up a Zoom Meeting, by first logging in to your Zoom account.

STEP 2: Hover your cursor over the "HOST A MEETING" button at the top-right corner of the screen, and select one of the following options:

- Screen Share Only
- With Video On
- With Video Off

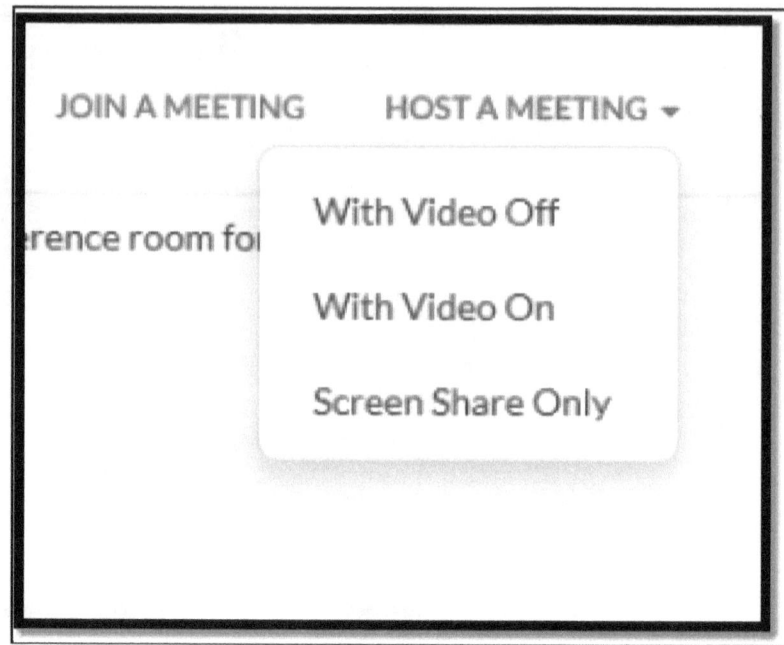

Step 3: The website will redirect you to the Zoom app and start a meeting. Here, you can edit meeting settings or copy the "Invitation URL" that you send to the attendees.

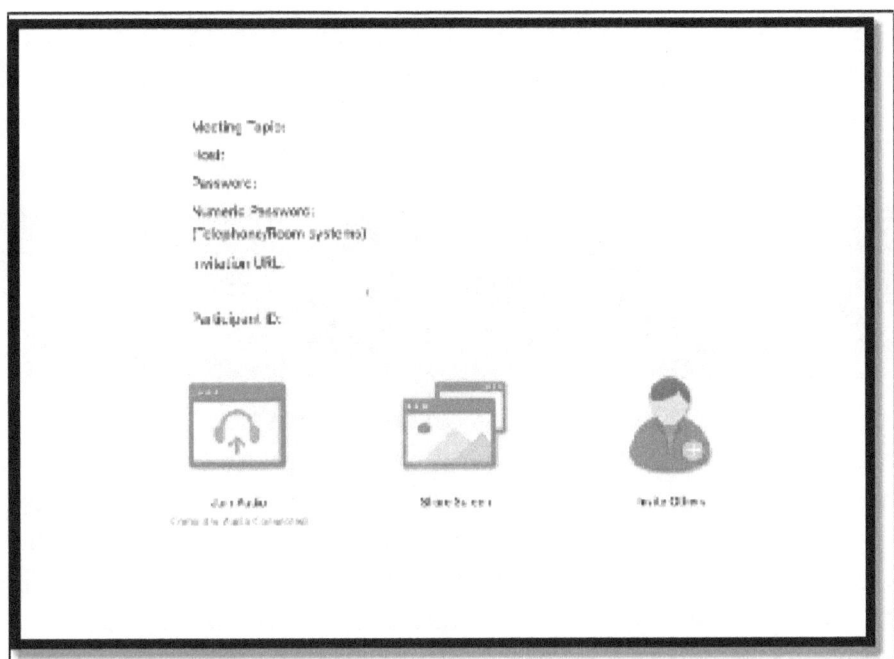

However, take note that you can also start a meeting quickly through the desktop app by following the instructions we listed for mobile devices later on.

USING MOBILE DEVICE (Starting A Zoom Meeting)

Step 1: Open the Zoom mobile app and sign in to your account.

Step 2: Tap the orange "New Meeting" icon that appears on your screen.

Step 3: Edit meeting settings according to your preferences (such as switching video off for participants, using a Personal Meeting ID, etc.) Check the procedure above (Zoom extra settings) if you havn't set it up. Once you're done, tap the blue "Start A Meeting" button. (**screenshot for starting a zoom meeting for mobile app**)

USING DESKTOP (Adding Participants to Zoom Meeting)

Step 1: For adding participant to a new meeting on the Zoom desktop app. In the new meeting screen, click on the "Invite" button in the toolbar at the bottom.

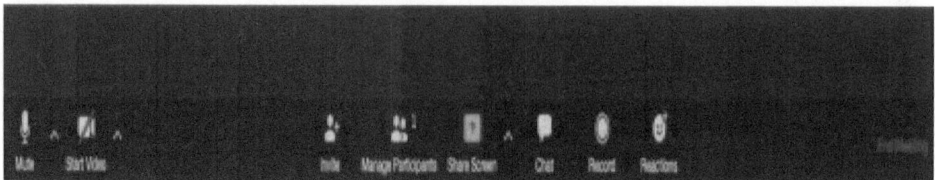

Step 2: Here, Zoom will give you the options to either Copy URL or Copy Invitation. You can send these to participants via text, email or instant messaging. However, there are another way to do this: through calendar invites. If you wish to invite others through a calendar, links to Google Calendar, Outlook Calendar, and Yahoo Calendar are displayed once your meeting has been saved.

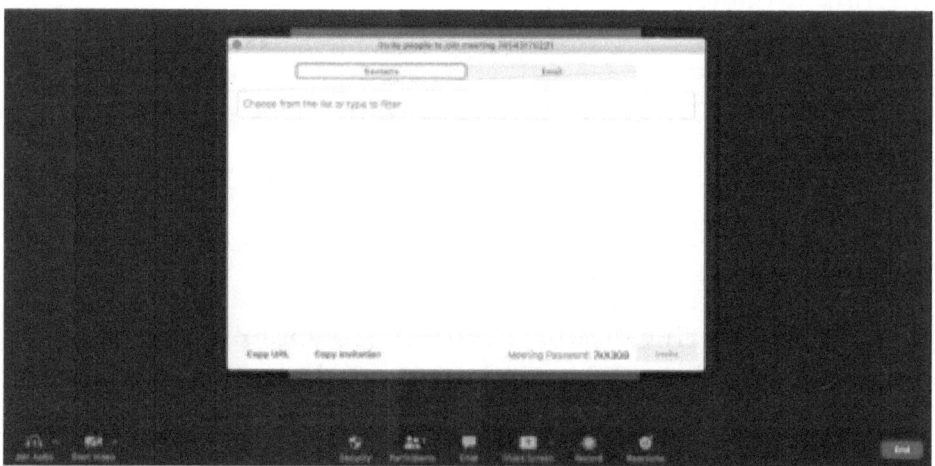

Step 3: You can also directly email the meeting details through your preferred email client via the Zoom app itself.

Using Mobile Device (Adding Participants to Zoom Meeting)

Step 1: Once the meeting starts, tap the "Participant" icon in the toolbar at the bottom of your screen to add and manage participants.

Step 2: In the Participants window that opens up, tap on the "Invite" option at the bottom left. Zoom will now give you the option to share your meeting details via a variety of communication platforms. These include various text, email and messaging apps on your smartphone. (**screenshot for starting a zoom meeting for mobile app**)

Joining Zoom Meeting

This is the guide to joining a Zoom meeting faster. Meanwhile, these steps are the same for both your desktop and your mobile devices.

BASIC STEP: Join Using A Meeting Link

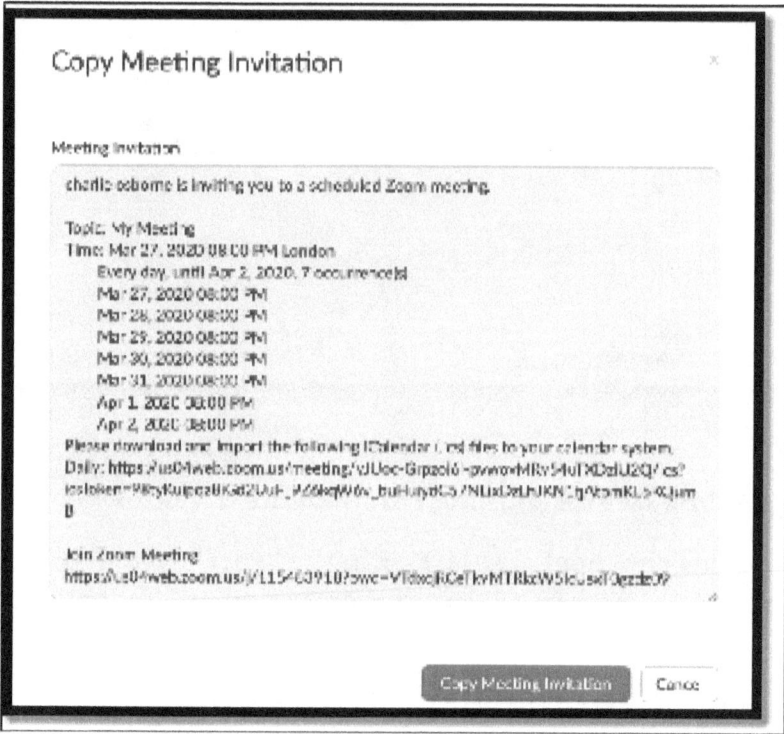

- If you have a meeting link, just can simply join by clicking on it.
- Or just copy and paste it into your web browser to join the meeting.

ADVANCE STEP: Join Using A Meeting ID

- Open the Zoom app and click on the "Join" icon.

- Paste the Meeting ID in the box provided, add your display name for the meeting and click on the "Join" button.

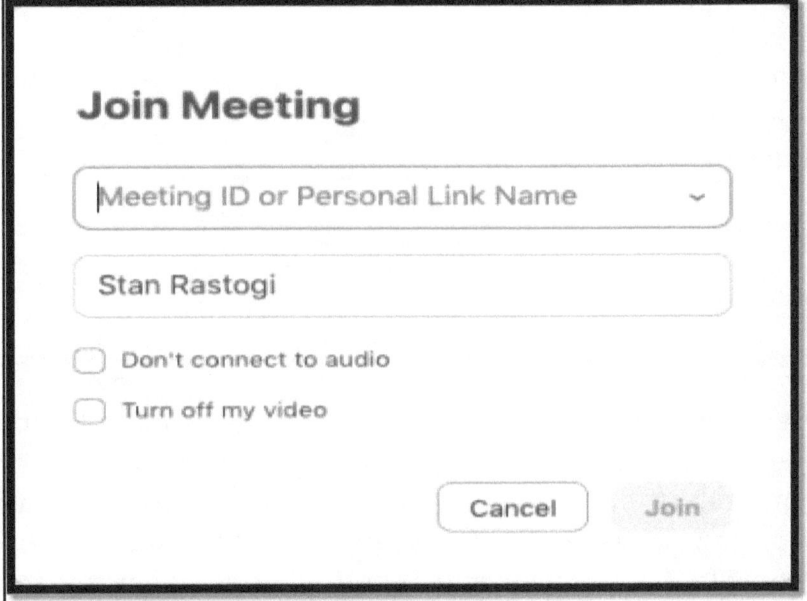

- You're now all set to communicate with your team members!

GUIDE TO SCHEDULING ZOOM MEETINGS

With your basic preferences in place of starting a zoom meeting, adding participants and joining zoom meeting, you can also easily schedule your upcoming Zoom meetings with these simple guides.

However, you can schedule your zoom meetings in this simple format; by going to the "Meetings" tab in your profile. The first screen you will see reveals any scheduled meetings in your diary. Click "schedule a new meeting" and a new screen will appear, in which you can name your meeting, add a description if you want, and choose the date or time.

Meanwhile, if this is to be a continual meet up with colleagues, there is a handy "recurring meeting" checkbox under the time-zone tab. If you select it, you can then choose how often the meeting needs to be repeated -- whether daily, weekly, and monthly. Luckily, Zoom lets you schedule meetings in advance to avoid this. Once you have input these details, scroll down and click "save."

FOR STEP BY STEP GUIDE TO SCHEDULING ZOOM MEETING:

USING DESKTOP

Step 1: To schedule a meeting, head to the Zoom app and click on the blue "Schedule" button (looks like a calendar icon).

Step 2: Enter meeting details in the Schedule Meeting pop up window that appears. You can set its date and time, privacy and access settings. You can also select your preferred calendar (between iCal, Google Calendar or others) to schedule the event in your calendar.

Schedule Meeting

Topic

[   ]

Date

[7/ 5/2020 ⌄] [5:00 PM ⌄] to [7/ 5/2020 ⌄] [5:30 PM ⌄]

◯ Recurring meeting   Time Zone: Mumbai, Kolkata, New Delhi ⌄

Meeting ID

◉ Generate Automatically   ◯ Personal Meeting ID 573-299-7884

Password

☑ Require meeting password [8xXS1P   ] ⑦

Video

Host ◯ On ◉ Off   Participants ◯ On ◉ Off

Audio

◯ Telephone ◯ Computer Audio ◉ Telephone and Computer Audio

Dial in from United States Edit

[Cancel]   [Schedule]

Step 3: Once you've adjusted preferences, click on the "Schedule" button at the bottom right of the screen.

Highly Recommended: Make sure you set a password because setting a meeting password can help avoid Zoombombing, which happens when someone who hasn't been invited to the meeting joins and disrupts it.

USING MOBILE DEVICES

Step 1: Login to your Zoom app.

Step 2: Go to the Meet & Chat homepage and click on the "Schedule" button.

Step 3: Enter the meeting name, date and time and click "Done."

Step 4: Zoom will redirect you or open another form for adding the event to your preferred calendar. Enter details like participant names and set the notifications into your calendar event, then tap "Done." You have now scheduled a Zoom meeting!

Furthermore, you can schedule meeting in your Learning Management System (LMS)

If you have a Learning Management System (LMS), Zoom's LTI Pro integration allows you to connect Zoom with your LMS and includes an extended feature set of what is offered in the basic LTI.

Step 1: Login to your LMS and go to the Zoom external tool link

Step 2: Click on the Schedule a Meeting button

Step 3: Enter in Topic, Date, and other related details and press Schedule. It is recommended that you make Registration required when scheduling a meeting, as that allows you to generate a registration report after the meeting is over.

STEPS TO RECORDING A ZOOM MEETINGS

Recording a meeting lets you easily use it as a reference to document everything that was discussed. This is especially important for remote teams who use Zoom video conferencing as their key mode of communication. Zoom allows you to record meetings easily and save it either to your local device or the

Zoom cloud. By saving it to the Zoom cloud, your team members can access it across multiple platforms easily.

Here's how to record Zoom meetings:

USING DESKTOP

Step 1: Start a meeting, in the Zoom toolbar, click on the "Record" icon.

Step 2: Choose between "Record on this Computer" or "Record to the Cloud." This automatically starts the recording.

Step 3: Click on "Pause/Stop Recording" to stop recording the meeting. Alternatively, you can also end a meeting to stop recording it.

Step 4: After you end the meeting, Zoom converts the recording to MP4 format and stores it in your preferred location. You can now easily access your recorded sessions any time you want!

USING MOBILE DEVICE

On mobile devices, Zoom lets you save meeting recordings only to the Zoom Cloud. Here's how to record a Zoom meeting using your mobile device:

Step 1: During a meeting, tap on the "More" option in the toolbar.

Step 2: Select the "Record to Cloud" feature to begin recording.

Step 3: You can pause or stop the recording by clicking the "More" button.

Step 4: After the meeting, you can find your recording in "My Recordings". You can access this section by logging into your Zoom account on a web browser.

Finally, the "End Meeting" tab finishes the session. If the host needs to leave but the meeting should carry on, they can assign the host status to another participant. But enabling co-hosts has to be selected first in the "Meetings" tab and can only be selected by subscription holders. Alternatively, you can leave the meeting or end the meeting for all.

CHAPTER 4: EDUCATIONAL ADMINIS-TRATIVE'S GUIDE TO MANAGING ZOOM

Zoom cares about our communities, businesses, schools, and all students. Zoom helps to have significantly increased educators' reliance on virtual learning environments. This administrational guide is mostly focused on school sector and little part of it for other organizations. We want to share with our valued educational customers best practices that can be implemented to ensure your company, school is using Zoom's services in ways that best promote the safety and privacy of the partners, students, teachers, and administrators who are your users. These best practices will help you create and maintain a safe and secure learning environment for your users. However, many of these practices will be applicable to webinar meetings and higher education institutions as well.

SUPERVISED ACCOUNT CREATION

Supervision of account creation is mainly for students under the age of 16. They should not go to zoom.us to create an account because;

- They should only be joining Zoom meeting sessions as participants (not separate account holders) through the School Subscriber's account
- Minors are not permitted to create an account per Zoom's Terms of Service. The School Subscriber's account administrator (e.g., teachers) should securely and confidentially provide meeting information and meeting passwords to the student users to ensure the school can maintain supervision and control over its student users' meeting experiences.

MSI OPTION

Account administrators can use this tool to mass configure the Zoom desktop client with the appropriate user settings and ensure those settings apply to each download with your school's account. For more information, please visit the links below: Link 1 https://support.zoom.us/hc/en-us/articles/201362163-Mass-Installation-and-Configuration-for-Windows and Link 2

https://support.zoom.us/hc/en-us/articles/115001799006-Mass-Deployment-with-Preconfigured-Settings-for-Mac

ONLY ALLOW USERS TO JOIN MEETINGS WITHIN YOUR ORGANIZATION'S ACCOUNT

If you issue student devices, you can lockdown the Zoom client to only allow users to join meetings from within your school's account. This ensures that Zoom can only be used for school related purposes.

Require Sign In To Account To Attend Meetings

Join Meeting

Meeting ID or Personal Link Name

Stan Rastogi

☐ Don't connect to audio

☐ Turn off my video

Cancel   Join

If using a school email address, enabling this setting requires users to login securely to participate in a meeting hosted by your school, ensuring that each meeting participant is monitored and identified. Meeting hosts can ensure that only registered and approved participants can attend a meeting.

Meeting Security and Controls Settings

The meeting host has a variety of controls they can use to secure their meeting. By default, Zoom has enabled the Waiting Room feature, required a meeting password, and set screen sharing to "Host Only" for a more secure meeting. However, by default the meeting security and controls;

• Prevent Participants from Screen Sharing: By default, only hosts are able to screen share to prevent disruptions. If you choose to allow others to share, the host can click the arrow next to Share Screen and click Advanced Sharing Options. Under "Who can share?" choose "All Participants" and close the window.

• Waiting Room: By default, waiting room has been enabled

which allows the host to control when a participant joins a meeting. When in a meeting, click manage participants and "Admit" to allow participants into your meeting.

• Meeting Password: By default, Zoom requires a meeting password for education. When creating a meeting, the password is embedded into the meeting/webinar links. When manually entering a meeting ID, the user will always be prompted to enter the password.

• Lock the Meeting: when you're in the meeting, click Participants at the bottom of your Zoom window. In the participants pop-up box, you will see a button that says Lock Meeting. When you lock the meeting, no new participants can join, even if they have the meeting ID and password.

• Expel a Participant: still in that participants menu, you can mouse over a participant's name, and several options will appear, including Remove. Click that to kick a participant out of the meeting. They can't get back in if you then click Lock Meeting.

• Attendee On-Hold: if you need a private moment, you can put attendees on-hold. The attendee's video and audio connections will be disabled momentarily. Click on the attendee's video thumbnail and select Start Attendee On-Hold to activate this feature.

•Disabling Video: Instructors can turn participant video off and request to start participant video. This will allow instructors to block unwanted, distracting or inappropriate gestures on video.

• Mute participants or Mute All: Instructors can turn mute / unmute participants or all. This will allow instructors to block unwanted, distracting or inappropriate noise from the meeting.

DISABLE PRIVATE CHAT

To ensure that students focus on the lesson at hand, meeting hosts can limit students' ability to chat amongst one another while a meeting is in session or in-meeting chat can be disabled in its entirety.

Disable Group Messaging Account-Wide

You can restrict the usage of Group Chat and Instant Messaging (out of meeting chat) or limit chat only to certain contacts such as Instructors or Counselors, restricting the possibility of students posting or disclosing any personal information to other students publicly. This can be done with IM groups.

TIPS FOR ADMINISTRATORS

1. How to Add Users to your Account

Option 1: Upload CSV File - You can add or update Zoom users by uploading a CSV file. You can also add users one at a time with user management.

Option 2: Managed Domains - You can set up your account to add existing users using your school's email address domain. Once set up, users with your specific domain will be prompted to join your account when they sign into Zoom.

Option 3: Single Sign On (SSO) - If your school uses SSO, this allows you to login using your company credentials.

2. How to communicate to Students

Option 1: Through your LMS (Schoology, Canvas, Blackboard, etc) - If using an LMS, you can set up your Zoom class meetings ahead of time that allows students and teachers to simply start and join Zoom meetings via a join link that is displayed on the LMS course, share cloud recording links to the course, and auto-provision Zoom users when they first access Zoom via your LMS. To get started visit: marketplace.zoom.us.

Option 2: Email/E-newsletter/Calendar - Utilize your email, e-newsletter, calendar, chat, or other online documents to send teachers, students, and guardians links to their recorded or live classes that you've scheduled with instructions for the day's lessons.

3. Tips and Tricks for Administrators and Staff

For Schoolwide Announcements:

- Utilize communication methods such as email, e-newsletter, chat, or other online documents to send teachers, students, and guardians links to their recorded or live classes that you've scheduled with instructions for the day's lessons.
- Conduct virtual morning announcements/assemblies to share the latest news and information about your school
- Host virtual staff meetings to check in with your staff and ensure they have the necessary resources and support.

For IT Support

- Any software or hardware related issues that teachers encounter can be resolved virtually through Zoom meetings, screen share, & remote desktop access

For Counseling Services

- Offer school counseling services to support students, teachers, and staff emotionally through difficult & stressful times.
- Guidance counselors can stay connected to high school juniors & seniors to help with college planning

For Professional Development

- Host training sessions with teachers to cover online learning strategies and to collaborate with their peers on best practices.

CHAPTER 5 - TEACHER'S GUIDE TO EDUCATING ON ZOOM

1. How to Host an Ad-hoc Meeting

- Start by opening your Zoom desktop app and clicking the Home button
- Press the New Meeting button.
- Once in the meeting, click the Participants button on the bottom of the screen then invite additional users.

2. Recording a Zoom Meeting

- When in a meeting, click the Record button.
- To access recording links, go to zoom.us/recording in your browser. You will be prompted to enter your login credentials if you are not logged into your Zoom account.
- Press the Share button next to the recording you'd like to distribute. You can update the sharing settings and distribute them using the provided link.

3. Delivering Virtual Instruction

Teaching Live using Zoom (Synchronous):

- Teachers can schedule Zoom meetings and post the meeting links in either their Learning Management System's classroom, or simply on an organized online document.
- Teachers and students will click on the meeting link at the appropriate time and conduct class as usual.

Recording Classes Via Zoom (Asynchronous):

- Start a Zoom meeting.

- Press the record button
- Teach your lesson
- End meeting, and send the link to the recording with detailed expectations including assignments. (When you share the meeting, click the box that says, "require registration" This will allow you to see who has viewed the video)

4. Commonly Used Control Settings in Zoom

Security Icon in Toolbar: Visible only to hosts and co-hosts of Zoom Meetings, the Security button provides easy access to several existing Zoom security features, as well as a new option to turn on the Waiting Room in-meeting. This button allows you to remove participants, lock your meeting, and decide if you want to allow your participants to screen share, chat, rename themselves, and annotate on shared content.

Managing Participants: As the host of a class/meeting, you can manage participants such as renaming, muting, stopping video and other controls for participants.

Video ON/OFF: Once in a meeting, you can turn your video on by clicking the "Start Video" icon on the bottom left of your screen. To turn it off, click the "Stop Video" icon.

Virtual background: Once in the meeting, you can select a virtual background by clicking the up caret to the right of the Start Video icon.

Speaker or Gallery view: At the top, you can pick one of two view options but this only impacts how you view a meeting, and not others. By default, Active Speaker is the default video layout in which the person talking is ramped up to a larger screen. But there is also a gallery layout which brings in every participant on one screen through a form of grid.

Muting: To ensure minimal background noise during your Zoom meeting, it is recommended that you mute everyone on the call when they're not talking. To do this, click on the Participants icon at the bottom of your screen click Mute All in the side panel.

CHAT IN A MEETING

- Meeting participants can ask questions during a Zoom Meeting via the meeting chat. Start by clicking the "Chat" icon on the bottom right of your screen.
- Once the chat panel will open up on the right, you can view and respond to all public chats.
- Use the three dots to choose whether you want to send messages to all meeting attendees or the host privately.
- However, be sure that Private chats will not be visible to the host. As a host, you can also select the "..." button to save a chat session and control who participants can talk to; no one, the host alone, everyone publicly, or everyone publicly and privately.

SHARING SCREEN

- Click the "Share Screen" icon at the bottom of your screen to share your desktop.
- If you'd like to share specific windows or applications, you can choose to do so from the dialog box.

CHAPTER 6 - ZOOM'S TIPS AND TRICKS

TEACHING OVER VIDEO

Tips and tricks for Virtual Lessons:

• For your first class, set aside some time to introduce your students to Zoom and ensure that they're able to connect their audio and video.

• Give an agenda or plan for each class by Screen Sharing a document or slide at the beginning of class. This gives students a clear idea of how the class will progress, what will be covered, and the activities they'll engage in.

• Discuss online etiquette and expectations of the students in your first virtual class and periodically revisit the topics.

• Utilize the Whiteboard or Annotate a shared document and let your students engage as well. When sharing a whiteboard, document, screen, or image, try whiteboarding math problems or have a student use annotation to highlight items such as grammar mistakes in a paper you're sharing.

• Take time to promote questions, comments, and reactions from your class. Give a minute to allow your students to utilize reactions, write their questions in chat, or be unmuted to ask their questions live.

• Divide into smaller groups for a discussion on a certain topic. You can use Zoom's Breakout Room feature to either pre-assign or auto-assign students into groups for a short period of time so they may discuss things together.

TIPS AND TRICKS FOR DELIVERY

• Pre-set your meeting to mute participant's microphones upon entry. This helps to avoid background noise and allow your students to focus on your lesson.

• Look at the camera to create eye contact with your students. This helps to create a more personal connection while teaching over video.

• Take a second to check chat or your student's video (if on camera) to check-in with your students and get feedback.

• Speak as if you're face-to-face with the class while ensuring you're at the appropriate distance from the microphone for the best audio experience.

• When delivering a presentation, sharing images, files or video, give your students a moment to open or take in what you've shared.

• Embrace the pause. Take a moment after the end of your comments and allow for students to engage before continuing on.

TIPS FOR EFFECTIVE VIDEO CONFERENCING

Most in-office teams might not be used to video conferencing and coping with the additional challenges it poses. To make your experience more comfortable, here are three tips that can help team members conduct seamless Zoom meetings and calls:

1. Always Mute Your Microphone Unless Speaking: Make sure to mute your microphone when you're not speaking. This eliminates any background noise or interference in the audio. To mute your microphone, use the microphone button at the bottom left of the Zoom toolbar that appears in the meeting screen.

Alternatively, you can set your Zoom meeting preferences to mute your microphone at the start of every meeting automatically.

To unmute yourself, use the microphone button or hold your spacebar for as long as you're speaking. This basic rule allows group meetings or conversations to run smoothly! For more efficient background noise elimination, use noise cancellation tools like Krisp to elevate your audio quality to the next level.

2. Inform Participants Before Recording The Meeting: Before you record any audio or video conference, make sure that all meeting participants are aware that they are being recorded and have permitted you to record them.

You could even take this permission in writing or record it at the start of the meeting. Why?

Not only does this maintain common courtesy, but it may be required by consent laws and regulations in many companies and regions.

3. Ensure Everything Is Working Correctly Before Starting A Meeting: It's extremely common for video conferences to be delayed or get interrupted due to technical snags. To ensure that this doesn't happen, turn on your device and check if Zoom's working correctly at least 10-15 minutes before every meeting. And if something's going wrong, alert your meeting host at the earliest (if you're the host – inform your participants of the same).

Meanwhile conducting a check before every meeting may feel tiring, it's far better than being embarrassed or annoyed when something goes wrong during your Zoom meeting!

More Advanced Tips

If you are using the desktop application, you can quickly access this area by going to "Settings" -- > "View More Settings." Under "Settings," select "In Meeting: Advanced," to find features including:

- Breakout room: Split meeting participants into separate, smaller rooms. This can also be done before a meeting begins to prevent logistics problems
- Remote support: Allows a host to provide 1:1 support to a participant
- Camera control: You can allow a participant to take remote control of your camera

- Show a "Join from your browser" link: a workaround for users that can't download Zoom software
- Invitation languages: You can choose from a variety of languages for meeting invitations, including English, Spanish, French, and Russian.
- Waiting room: a feature to keep participants in a 'waiting area' until the host is ready for them -- particularly handy for remote interviews or office hours. This feature is now on as default for education, Basic, and single-license Pro accounts.

CHAPTER 7 - ZOOM'S SPECIAL FEATURES

You now know how to use Zoom Meetings and so many other important areas in Zoom. However, I still want to give more details about these additional features in Zoom even though I have discussed a little about them.

Here's a detailed about these additional Zoom's special features and how to use them effectively.

1. SCREEN SHARING

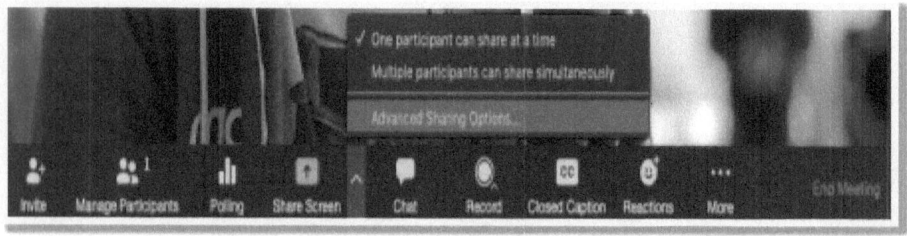

Zoom lets you share your screen with other meeting participants easily.

This lets you:

- Host virtual presentations and workshops.
- Explain processes in detail.
- Review work and project documents together with your team.

To share your screen, just click on the "Share Screen" icon in the toolbar.

This lets you share:

- A specific app or window.

- A whiteboard.
- Apple iPhone / iPad screen (if your device supports this).

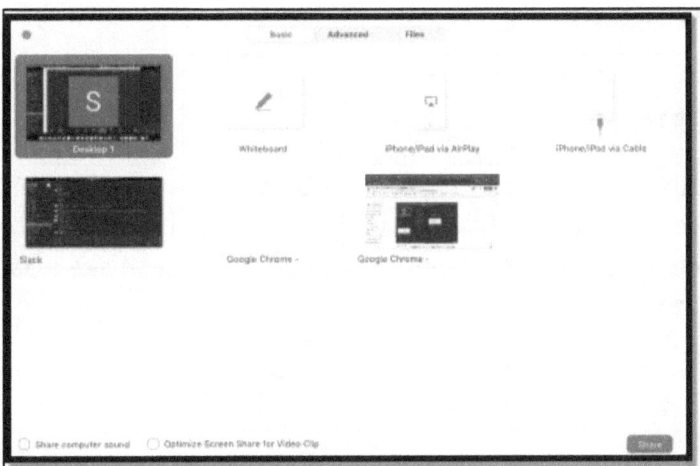

If you want more screen sharing options, click on the "Advanced" tab at the top of your screen. Here, you can choose to share:

- A part of your screen or the entire screen.
- Only your computer's sound or your microphone's sound as well.
- Content from a second camera or content only from your screen.

There is also a file-sharing tab under "share screen" (shown under "Files"), which includes application links to Dropbox, Microsoft OneDrive, Google Drive, and Box. As a host, you can also use the arrow next to the "Share Screen" tab to control whether participants are limited to one screen share at a time, or alternatively, you can give permission for multiple screens to be shared at once.

2. ZOOM WEBINARS

If you have a Pro, Business, or Enterprise plan, you can take advantage of the webinars option. Webinars can be set up that broadcast to up to 10,000 view-only attendees at a time. Screens, video, and audio can be shared; chat sessions between attendees and panelists can be hosted, and webinars can be run on either a pre-registration or open basis.

3. ZOOM PHONE

Zoom Phone uses the Voice over Internet Protocol (VoIP) to help you make Zoom calls over the cloud. This is similar to calling from a phone number, except that the calls here are hosted over the internet.

Zoom Phone comes with plenty of additional features to make your calling experience seamless.

These include:

- Integration with CRMs like Salesforce.
- Call conferencing and delegation.
- Call recording and voice mail features.

However, Zoom Phone isn't available with the standard pricing plans. Instead, you must pay for it separately. Prices start at $10/ user per month and require you to have at least one paid licensed host.

4. ZOOM WHITEBOARDS

Earlier, we mentioned the "whiteboard" option under the "Share Screen" tab. This is a useful option if you are canvassing ideas or soliciting feedback and it comes with different annotation options, including text boxes, arrows, and more. The "spotlight" is a form of highlighter which can be used to bring user attention to a particular area or point.

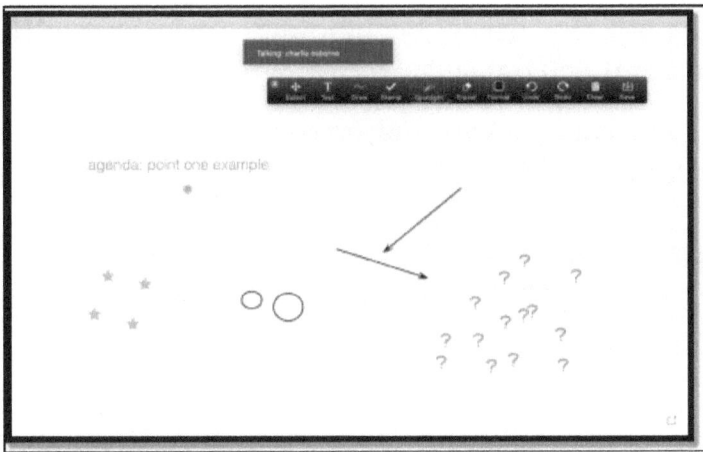

5. ZOOM ROOMS

Zoom Rooms are essentially virtual conference rooms where only particular members have access. You can use these rooms for various purposes such as:

- Video conferencing
- Audio conferencing
- Screen sharing

Zoom Rooms offer various features, such as:

- One-touch sharing and conferencing.
- Use up to 12 whiteboards at a time.
- Digital signage/display around an office.

This usually requires additional hardware (multiple webcams, connectors, monitors, etc.) as well as conference room design considerations. Like Zoom Phone, Zoom Rooms aren't available in the standard pricing plans but must be purchased additionally at $49/room per month.

6. ZOOM VIRTUAL BACKGROUNDS

Virtual backgrounds can be used to hide the chaos and clutter of your home. There are specific hardware requirements, which can be accessed here. Most modern PC setups should be able to manage but the virtual background works best with a green screen and uniform lighting.

To set up a virtual background, go to the desktop app, "Settings," and choose "Virtual Background." You will be prompted to download a virtual background package, just once and then you can try out different screens or add your own image/video instead. You may see a warning that says your hardware isn't good enough but give it a go, anyway.

CHAPTER 8 - ZOOM SECURITY TABS

The security tab is all about preventing Zoom gatecrashers from invading your Zoom events. The features help keep off uninvited guests out of Zoom.

Further details about Zoom gatecrashers and how to prevent it;

When software becomes popular; it has scammers come out of the woodwork to try and find a way to capitalize. Zoom is no different; the appearance of scammers jumping into unprotected meetings and posting malicious links and pornography has given rise to the phrase "Zoom-bombing."

The problem has become common enough for Zoom to publish a guide on how to prevent gatecrashers from disrupting your meetings, including pointers such as:

- Keep your meeting links off social media
- Do not use your Personal Meeting ID (PMI) to host public events. Instead, generate a random ID.
- Choose "only host" for screen sharing control during a meeting

- Only allow signed-in users to join a meeting
- Use the "lock" feature to prevent random users from joining in. You might also want to consider using the Waiting Room.
- If you are gatecrashed, hover over the user's name in the Participants menu to bring up a "remove" option.

ZOOM SECURITY

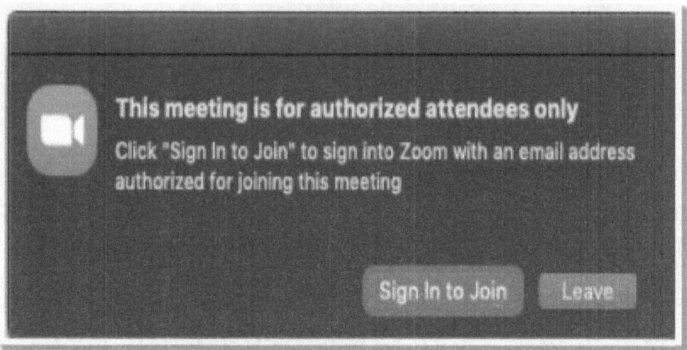

Since the video conferencing software's popularity exploded, the vendor has been playing catch-up to improve the security of the software, together with the help of researchers and security experts. The company has introduced a range of new measures, including:

- Permitting meeting hosts to configure minimum meeting password requirements
- Changing the 9-digit setup for randomly-generated meeting IDs to 11 digits
- Removing Facebook's iOS SDK client to stop unnecessary data collection
- Removing attendee attention tracker features
- Resolving vulnerabilities in the Zoom installer and Windows client
- Using personal meeting IDs (PMIs) can now be disabled

- Showing profile pictures can be disabled
- An expiration date for cloud recordings can be set, as well as whether or not they can be shared

Zoom has also announced the acquisition of Keybase. Zoom has been using a substandard AES-128 key in ECB mode, but paid users may eventually be able to use end-to-end encryption on their calls.

Also, the latest version of Zoom, version 5.0, will become a forced upgrade for users. Users will not be able to join calls unless they upgrade. The reason for this is that Zoom 5.0 implements AES-256 GCM encryption, an upgrade from the substandard key.

Zoom 5.0 Features includes:

- Support for AES 256-bit GCM encryption and a new icon to show the security measure is in place
- A 'report user' function
- Meeting hosts can choose the data center region they wish to connect to
- The option to 'end' or 'leave' a meeting -- making to easier to close down the session or choose a new host with meeting privileges

CHAPTER 9 - ZOOM ALTERNATIVES

If you really having issues using Zoom or fully not satify with the App, there are still other alternatives provided for you in this book and they are simply easy to use too. They include;

- **Discord:** It has emerged as a strong alternative to Zoom, thanks to its video conferencing capabilities that let you connect with up to 50 participants at once. The platform is popular amongst gamers, though you can use it as a tool to communicate with your office team or some friends. You can also download its mobile app to connect with your contacts using your smartphone. There are also features to share your screen or perform voice calls. Just like other free alternatives to Zoom, Discord provides video conferencing at no cost. All you just need is to sign up on the Discord site or through its app to get started with your virtual conferences.

- **Skype:** It has been around since 2003, making it a great and reliable way to stay connected with others.

Whether you want to have a quick work meeting, host an interview call, or just check in with your friends, Skype is a viable option that allows up to 50 people in a phone or video call. Plus, online calls are free. Skype is the easier option, mostly because people are usually already familiar with the software, whereas Zoom is something many people are just now starting to figure out.

- **Cisco Webex Meetings:** Cisco is offering free access to its Webex Meetings in all countries where it is available to support the work from home needs during the coronavirus outbreak. Despite being available as free, you'll get all enterprise features including unlimited usage with no time restrictions, support for up to 100 participants, and a toll dial-in in addition to Voice-over-Internet-Protocol (VoIP) capabilities. All you need is to sign up on the Cisco Webex portal to get started with the Webex Meetings. Overall, the experience that's been offered by Cisco is nowhere limited when comparing with Zoom.

- **Microsoft Teams:** Microsoft Teams is a great option for businesses, especially if a lot of your work is already done using Microsoft Suite. It's a way to consistently use the same platform for all of your work. Video calls can host up to 250 members and is a great option for those who want to have work or class presentations. While it shares a lot of similar Zoom features, including file sharing, screen sharing, and text chats along with video calls, Microsoft Teams is more suitable to those who want to keep their all of their professional work in one place.

"Great things in business are never done by one person;
they are done by a team of people." — Steve Jobs